by Joanne Mattern

illustrated by Donna Reynolds

ISBN 0-8167-7482-X

Printed in Canada.

10 9 8 7 6 5 4 3 2 1

Icky Introduction

It's icky. It's sticky. It's gooey. What is it? Slime!

Our world is a slimy place. There are slimy animals and plants. There's even slime in your body, because the human body is one of the slimiest things on Earth.

This book may not look slimy, but it's filled with cool scientific facts about all kinds of slippery, sticky stuff. So take a deep breath and prepare to get slimed!

Nice to Eat You

Plants are pretty harmless life-forms, right? Not necessarily. Several strange plants have a slimy and deadly way of finding food. These plants eat insects by *digesting them alive.*

There are several different kinds of *insectivorous,* or insect-eating, plants. You may have heard of the Venus's-flytrap. This plant can grow about a foot tall and has small, white flowers. But it's the leaves that are the slimiest part of the plant. A Venus's-flytrap's leaves are divided into two halves that fit together like a clamshell. Each half is lined with long, sharp spines.

The Venus's-flytrap produces a liquid that smells sweet. Insects crawl onto the leaves to get some of this yummy-smelling slime. Bad idea! When an insect touches a sensitive hair inside a Venus's-flytrap's leaf—snap! The leaf slams shut, trapping the insect between those sharp spines.

That's when things get really slimy. Digestive fluids inside the plant begin to break down the insect's body. After the insect is digested, the Venus's-flytrap opens up again and waits for another meal.

Some people keep Venus's-flytraps as pets. Along with feeding their plants live insects, these folks also drop in bits of hamburger and other meat for a slimy snack.

The pitcher plant is another insect-eating plant. But the pitcher plant has a different way of catching its prey. This plant's leaves are shaped like pitchers (the kind that hold water, not the baseball kind!). They also have downward-pointing hairs on their inside surface. When an insect crawls onto a pitcher plant leaf, it slides down the hairs to the bottom. What's waiting down there? A slimy little pool of digestive juices. In a short time, that insect is lunch.

Then there is the sundew. These plants look pretty, with their little clusters of pink, purple, or white flowers. But watch out for those leaves! Each leaf is covered with little hairs coated in gooey fluid. When an insect lands on the leaf, it gets trapped in the sticky hairs. Once the hairs have captured their prey, they curl inward and hold the unlucky insect. Then those slimy digestive juices get to work, digesting the insect and feeding the plant.

Most insectivorous plants are found in bogs. Bogs are pretty slimy places themselves, with lots of water and rotting vegetation. Because bogs have poor soil for growing plants, insectivorous plants count on insects to provide them with the protein they need to grow.

Slimy Neighborhoods

Imagine a place where slime covers your feet as you walk. In some spots, the ground might give way under your feet, plunging you even deeper into slime. These places are found all over the world. They are called wetlands.

Wetlands come in a variety of types and have different names. Some, such as swamps and marshes, are low-lying areas where there's a great deal of water in the soil. The ground in swamps and marshes is wet, muddy, and slimy.

But the slimiest places of all are bogs. Bogs are wet areas that contain a great deal of decomposing plant matter called *peat*. In Ireland and other parts of the world, people cut up peat, dry it, and burn it as fuel.

Because grass and other plants grow in bogs, the ground can look solid enough to walk on. But watch out! The ground is so waterlogged that it can't support much weight. People who lived long ago laid planks across the bogs or used stepping stones to make safe paths to walk on. One false step and you could end up buried to your neck in slime!

The rotting plants in bogs produce a kind of acid that is excellent for preserving dead bodies. Hundreds of bodies have been found in bogs around the world. These

bodies are often incredibly well preserved. In 1978, the body of a woman was found in a bog in Donegal, Ireland. Scientists determined that the woman had died around the year 1570. Even though it had been buried in the wet bog for more than four hundred years, the woman's body still had most of its skin. It also had hair and eyelashes. Her clothes had been preserved as well.

Bodies end up in bogs for several different reasons. Some bodies may have been those of unlucky travelers who sank into the bog while trying to cross the watery ground. Other bodies might have belonged to people who were sacrificed and buried there as part of ancient religious rituals.

Slimy Insects

You've probably shooed a few flies away from your food. You might think these bugs are annoying. But flies are more than annoying. They are slimy and disgusting!

Flies are always hanging around food. This might not seem like a big deal until you find out what those flies are doing on food that might be going into your mouth! When a fly lands on food, it vomits on it. Yuck! This slimy vomit contains digestive juices from the fly's stomach. Then the fly uses its tongue to lick up the vomit and the food, before flying away to find something else to eat. Now, are you still hungry for that potato chip a fly just landed on?

Flies have to vomit on their food because it's the only way they can eat. These insects don't have teeth or mouth parts that can suck or bite. Instead, they vomit up digestive juices to make solid food—such as sandwiches, cookies, or French fries—gooey enough to eat. And flies eat almost anything, from cookies to dead animals to dog poop. Double yuck!

Another slimy thing about flies is their feet. Flies can walk up walls and across ceilings because their feet are covered with tiny hairs. These hairs are coated with a gooey liquid that helps flies stick to whatever surface they're walking on. Unfortunately, germs and dirt and

other nasty things also stick to the hairs. That's why flies are responsible for spreading so many diseases. If a fly picks up germs from a piece of garbage, then walks on the apple you're about to bite into, those germs will spread to the apple and then go into your body, where they might make you sick.

Unfortunately, flies are so small that you can't see all the slimy, sickening things they do to your food. This is one case where what you don't know *can* hurt you!

⁂

Mosquitoes are another big disease-spreader. But the mosquito doesn't spread disease by vomiting or walking around with its slimy little feet. Instead, the mosquito sucks blood. Just think of the mosquito as the vampire of the insect world. These insect vampires have killed more people on Earth than any movie monster ever could.

Actually, it's only the female mosquito that's dangerous. The male mosquito can't hurt anyone. He has a small mouth and drinks only water and the sweet nectar produced by flowers. But the female mosquito has a large, sharp mouth that's especially made to pierce the skin and suck blood.

When a mosquito bites, she spits some slimy saliva into the wound to make the blood flow more quickly and easily. The saliva also makes the skin swollen and itchy, which is why mosquito bites are so annoying.

A mosquito is tiny, so there's no way she can suck enough blood out of a person to kill him or her. However, a mosquito's bite can spread terrible diseases, such as malaria, yellow fever, and West Nile virus. So many people have died of mosquito-spread diseases through the ages that these little insects are considered the deadliest animals in the world. Scientists think that mosquitoes alone have caused *half* of all human deaths in history.

Other insects don't chow down on people. They eat each other instead. Say hello to the giant water bug, which may live in a pond or lake near you. This insect has long, flat legs, which it uses to "row" through the water like a boat. The water bug also uses its legs to push it deep under the water. As it swims and dives, it looks for frogs, fish, insects, or tadpoles to eat.

When the water bug spots some dinner, it sneaks up on its prey and grabs it with its powerful legs. Then it bites the animal with its long, sharp mouth parts. That's when things get really gross. The bug's mouth parts are like a straw. Once it sticks them into its prey, it starts to suck. The water bug actually sucks the insides out of the other animal, until its prey's body is empty.

⁂

Let's get back on dry land for a while. Are there any slimy, weird insects here? You bet!

During the summer, you may hear an insect called the cicada buzzing in the trees. The male cicadas are looking for females to mate with. What they *don't* want to attract is a type of wasp known as the cicada killer.

When this wasp catches a cicada, it stings it. The sting paralyzes the cicada but doesn't kill it. Something worse happens next.

Once the wasp has paralyzed its victim, it brings the cicada back to its underground nest. Then it lays eggs inside the paralyzed cicada's body. When the wasp eggs hatch, the larvae feed on the cicada. Those baby wasps actually eat the cicada alive!

⁂

The ichneumon is another insect that sucks the life out of its living prey. These insects lay their eggs inside another insect's larvae or eggs. When the ichneumon eggs hatch, they start munching on their helpless host. While this is bad news for the prey, it can be good news for people, because many of the insects that ichneumons eat are harmful to crops.

Bloodsuckers

How about a nice glass of blood for dinner? If you were a leech, a tick, or a vampire bat, it would be a tasty treat!

Leeches look slimy, and they do slimy things. These worms are also called bloodsuckers, and with good reason. Sucking blood is how a leech finds food!

Leeches live in the water. When a warm-blooded animal or person swims or wades past, the leech grabs on with its powerful suckers. Then it bites into the skin with its razor-sharp teeth, spits some saliva into the wound to keep the blood flowing, and starts sucking. A leech can suck blood for several hours. By the time it's finished, its thin body is round and fat. Then the leech drops off and digests all that tasty blood. It may be several months before it's hungry again. Leeches can suck nine times their weight during one meal. Most leeches are small, but a few kinds grow to about 18 inches long. That's a lot of blood sucking!

Believe it or not, some people deliberately put leeches on themselves so the worms can suck their blood. Why? Long ago, doctors used leeches to suck out "bad blood" that they thought made people sick. Today, doctors sometimes use leeches to help patients who have had operations to reattach fingers or other body parts. Often, the blood does not flow well through reattached body parts. Having a leech grab on and suck out some of the blood helps the body heal faster. So some slimy creatures are actually good for you—if used the right way, of course!

Other times, blood-sucking creatures can be bad indeed. Take the tick, for example. This tiny creature eats only three times during its two-year life span. Unfortunately, there's only one thing on the menu—blood.

Ticks usually live in long grass or wooded areas. When an animal or a person walks by, the tiny tick jumps on. It bites its unsuspecting host, injects some slimy spit into the wound, and starts sucking. As it fills with blood, the tick's body gets bigger . . . and bigger . . . and bigger! If you squeezed the tick's body hard enough, it would pop like a blood balloon. Gross!

It's important to remove ticks from yourself or your pets as soon as you see them, because many ticks spread diseases such as Rocky Mountain spotted fever and Lyme disease. The best way to get rid of a tick is to grab its body with a pair of tweezers and pull it out, slowly and firmly. But don't yank! If you do, the tick's head—which is buried under the skin—might come off and stay inside you or your pet's body.

You've probably seen old vampire movies where the blood-sucking vampire changes into a bat and flies away into the night. There really is a kind of bat that sucks blood. Not surprisingly, its name is the vampire bat.

Vampire bats are active at night. Their prey is usually

cattle or pigs. The bat flies over to a sleeping animal and bites its ears or feet with its sharp teeth. The bite doesn't hurt, at least not enough to wake the sleeping prey. Then the bat laps up the blood with its tongue. On rare occasions, people become meals for vampire bats. Although a vampire bat doesn't take enough blood to kill an animal or a person, its bite can spread deadly diseases, including rabies.

Why do some animals drink blood, anyway? Blood is a great source of protein and iron, two nutrients that animals—and people—need to survive.

Slime Underwater

You would think an animal that lives underwater would be clean. Actually, there are several underwater dwellers that are slimy—*very* slimy.

The hagfish is one of the slimiest creatures on Earth. The hagfish's body isn't much more than a tube of slime. This creature is brown or gray, shaped like a worm, and about 3 feet long. It has tiny eyes, a big mouth, and only one tooth. A few tentacles grow around the mouth to help the fish find food.

But the most unpleasant thing about the hagfish is the thick layer of mucus that covers its body. A hagfish is so slimy that if you put one in a bucket of water and check back a few hours later, you'll find mucus floating on top of the water.

Where does all this slime come from? The hagfish has mucous glands all over its body. These glands secrete mucus all the time. It's like having a constantly runny nose! And if the hagfish becomes upset or scared, watch out! Even more mucus gushes out of its body. This slimy stuff protects the body of the fish. It also probably tastes disgusting to predators, who will quickly leave the hagfish alone and go find something tastier—and not quite so slimy!—to eat.

Speaking of eating, hagfish have some slimy digestive

habits, too. Hagfish are terrible swimmers and spend most of their time slithering through the mud at the bottom of the sea. When a hagfish finds a sick or dead fish, it attaches its lips to the fish's eyeball or gills. Then it pokes a hole in its prey with its single tooth and starts sucking. By the time the hagfish is done slurping out the fish's insides, there is nothing left of the prey except the skin and the bones. One kind of hagfish can eat eighteen times its weight in just seven hours.

The hagfish has a slimy relative called the lamprey. Lampreys are long fish with a big, round mouth at one end. This mouth is full of sharp teeth and a tongue that is covered with even more spiky teeth.

Like hagfish, lampreys use the grab-and-suck method of eating. The lamprey attaches itself to the skin of a passing fish, animal, or person. Its teeth bite down, and saliva flows into the wound to keep the blood from clotting. Then the lamprey sucks blood until it is full. Many fish die from lamprey bites that become infected.

There's one more underwater creature that deserves to be in the Slime Hall of Fame. That's the starfish. Starfish, or sea stars, are some of the weirdest animals on Earth! They have no head and no brain. Five or more arms grow out from a central nerve disk, and each arm is covered with tiny, suction cup–like feet. Starfish are bumpy or spiky, and come in many different colors.

The weirdest thing about a starfish is the way it digests food. Starfish have a tiny mouth and a big stomach. The creature's mouth is so small that it can't bite, chew, or swallow. Instead, when a starfish finds a clam or a piece of coral to eat, it vomits its stomach out of its mouth and starts digesting its prey on the spot! Slimy chemicals turn the prey into a wet, squishy blob. Then the starfish sucks its prey into its stomach, pulls its stomach back into its body, and goes on its merry way.

Shooting Slime

One sea creature has a gross secret weapon: its own slimy guts!

The sea cucumber is a slippery creature that lives in the ocean. The outside of its body is covered with slimy mucus. In some species, this mucus is poisonous. But that's nothing compared with this creature's slimy insides—and the way it uses them to defend itself.

When the sea cucumber is scared or threatened, it can shove its intestines and stomach out of its body through its rear end! The intestines and stomach are sticky and messy, and do a great job of entangling the attacker. Sometimes, the intestines just wiggle around on the ground to distract the predator. Meanwhile, the sea cucumber crawls away safely. Soon afterward, it grows a whole new stomach and intestines. Now there's a trick to try at parties!

Sometimes, sea cucumbers don't attack other animals with their intestines. Instead, they squirt long threads out of their rear ends. These slimy threads wrap themselves around the attacker. What a way to defend yourself!

Even though sea cucumbers are unattractive, they are a popular food in Asia. Sea cucumbers can be sliced up and dried. Sometimes they are made into a soup. *Bon appétit!*

My Pet Slime

Would you keep slime for a pet? You could if you had a slime mold!

Slime molds are weird. They're neither animals nor plants. They aren't even molds. They are part of a special group of living things called *Protoctista*.

A slime mold is just one huge cell. Usually, cells are microscopic. But a slime mold often grows up to 6 inches around. Some are even bigger. The largest slime mold ever found was 3 feet wide and 30 feet long! If a slime mold is divided into smaller pieces, each piece can grow into a new cell.

Slime molds are gooey creatures that look a bit like Jell-O®. They come in different colors. Slime molds move more slowly than a glacier and eat bacteria and other microscopic creatures. They like damp places, such as under fallen trees and leaves.

Obviously, slime molds aren't as cuddly as kittens or as playful as puppies. But would you believe that some people really do keep them as pets? A woman named Ruth Nauss took her pet slime molds on vacation with her. She even used hot water bottles to keep them warm on cold nights. One of her slime molds lived for nine years.

Slimy Slugs and Snails

Quick, think of a slimy animal! A slug or a snail might have just popped—or slithered—into your mind.

Snails live inside hard shells. Although the shell is hard and dry, what's inside is slimy. A snail's body is covered with mucus. It moves by crawling along on a large, muscular foot on the bottom of its body. This foot is covered with slimy mucus to help the snail ooze along the ground.

Slugs are even slimier than snails. These gooey creatures don't have a shell. But like snails, slugs squirt mucus onto the bottom of their bodies to help them crawl. The slime helps them slide over rocks, thorns, and other sharp objects without getting hurt. Slugs can even slither their way up trees. And some slugs make a rope out of mucus that squirts out their rear end. Then the slug hangs from its slime rope to get down from trees or other high places. Whee!

The bottom of a slug's body isn't the only slimy thing about this creature. Slugs have mucus *all over* their bodies. This mucus may be slimy and gross, but it helps the slug survive. Without that protective covering of slime, the slug's body would dry out and it would die.

Slime also helps a slug defend itself. When a slug is attacked, it releases extra mucus—up to a third of its body weight in slime! Most predators don't think a slimy, slippery slug tastes good, and they usually leave the creature alone.

A slug's slime also provides a home for other creatures. Slugs are often covered with teeny-tiny mites that live in the mucus.

Some slugs live in water. Others live on land. Garden slugs are small and usually grayish-white. The banana slug is yellow and larger, and looks a lot like the fruit it's named after. The largest land slug is the European slug, which can be up to a foot long. That's a lot of slime!

When slugs mate, the first thing they do is squirt out lots of slime. Sometimes, they eat each other's slime to get acquainted. Every slug is both male and female. (Snails,

too.) So when two slugs mate with each other, both get pregnant! Soon after, they will lay lots of gooey eggs.

Some people dislike slugs. For example, many gardeners hate these slimy creatures because they munch on plants with their tooth-covered tongues. Some gardeners kill slugs by shaking salt on them. The salt draws the moisture out of the slug's body until the creature dries up and dies.

But other people think slugs are cool. The banana slug is the mascot of the University of California at Santa Cruz. Students there wear the slug with pride on their T-shirts. They are proud to be slimy!

Slime in the Soil

Imagine a slimy creature that crawls through the dirt. This creature eats dirt as it moves under the ground, then excretes waste material out its other end. What kind of animal is this? An earthworm! These wiggly, slimy creatures are everywhere in the earth. One acre of farmland can contain millions of worms.

Worms have slime-covered bodies to keep them from drying out. The slime also makes it easier for the worms to move, which is helpful because they don't have any feet!

Gardeners love earthworms because they make the soil healthy. As an earthworm tunnels through the ground, it helps air and water move through the soil. Worm excrement is also a good source of nutrients for plants.

Have you ever seen worms covering the sidewalk after it rains? Worms come out of the ground when it rains because their tunnels fill up with water. They also like the moisture of all those puddles and wet spots. But they have to be careful when the sun comes out! If the worm doesn't get back underground before the puddles disappear, its slimy coating will dry up and the worm will die.

Worms can come in super sizes. The Gippsland earthworm, which lives in Australia, can be up to 12 feet long and weigh 1.5 pounds. But that's nothing compared with a worm that was found in South Africa. That bad boy was 22 feet long!

Pass the Slime, Please!

How would you like to eat vomit and slime every day for breakfast, lunch, and dinner? Sounds horrible to us, but there are lots of animals that do just that.

Baby birds often get all of their nutrition from food that their parents regurgitate, or vomit. Doves, finches, herons, and penguins are just a few of the birds that do this. Although you wouldn't like to find regurgitated worm guts on your plate at dinnertime, this feeding arrangement works well for birds. Baby birds eat almost all day long. It's easier and more efficient for parent birds to feed their kids regurgitated food than to fly off every few minutes to find another worm or insect to eat. It's also easier for young birds to digest food that has already been partly digested by Mom or Dad.

Vomited food can also be a sign of romance. Before two gulls mate, they often regurgitate food for each other. How sweet!

⋔ ⋔ ⋔

You've probably seen cows chewing their cuds. Did you know that they are actually chomping on regurgitated food?

Cows are part of a group called ruminants. Deer, goats, camels, antelope, and sheep are also ruminants. Ruminants have unusual stomachs with three or four sections. A cow's stomach is huge—as big as nine human stomachs! Ruminants need this special stomach because they eat grass, which is hard to digest.

When a cow eats a mouthful of grass, it goes right into the first part of the stomach without being chewed up first. This part of the stomach is called the rumen. The rumen is filled with digestive juices containing billions of tiny bacteria. The bacteria get to work turning the grass into a gooey, chewy wad called a cud.

A few hours later, the cow coughs up the cud and starts chewing. Along with those slippery digestive juices from the rumen, the cow adds the saliva in its mouth. A cow can produce almost 846 cups of saliva in one day!

After plenty of chewing, the cud goes back down into a different part of the cow's stomach. More slimy digestive juices get to work there. The cud moves through the remaining two sections of the stomach and the rest of the cow's digestive system until all the nutrients are taken out. The leftover waste material is excreted.

Hairball Mania

Have you ever had a pet cat? If so, you probably know that cats throw up. Sometimes cats throw up partly digested food. But more often all that coughing and hacking brings up a hairball.

Hairballs look like wet, furry pink lumps. When cats groom themselves, they swallow a lot of hair. Since hair isn't food, it needs to get out of the cat's body. Usually, the best way to do this is to regurgitate the hairball. Because it's been in the cat's stomach, the hair is often mixed with partly digested food and looks slimy and soft.

Hairballs aren't good for cats, and they aren't great for the carpet either! To keep cats from getting so many hairballs, some owners feed them gooey medicine made of petroleum jelly or mineral oil. When cats eat the jelly, it mixes with the hairballs and makes them slimy. Then it's easier for the hairball to be excreted the normal way.

Owls spit up a kind of hairball, too, called an owl pellet. Owl pellets aren't made of owl feathers. They contain the fur and bones of the owl's prey.

When owls chow down, they eat *everything!* That means when an owl catches a mouse for dinner, it swallows the whole creature headfirst. Forget about chewing or removing yucky things like bones. Everything

goes straight into the owl's stomach, where digestive juices turn the mouse into nutrients and waste material. Some of the waste leaves the bird's body the normal way. But things like fur, feathers, bones, claws, and teeth are clumped together in a pellet. A few hours later, the owl spits out the pellet. Dinner is done!

Owl pellets actually can be useful to some animals and humans. Some moths and beetles use the material in owl pellets to build cocoons or as a place to lay eggs. Scientists collect other pellets. They take the pellets apart to discover what the owl has eaten. One scientist studied 200 pellets from one owl and found 412 mice, 20 shrews, 20 rats, a mole, and a sparrow! It's a slimy job, but somebody has to do it!

Super Slimy Animal Facts

Here are some things that may surprise you about slimy animal behavior!

- Animal blood comes in different colors. Insects may have green, yellow, or clear blood because there isn't any iron in it. (Iron is what gives human blood its red color.) A cockroach's blood is white. Lobsters, crabs, shrimps, and some spiders, snails, and slugs have blue blood because their blood contains copper.
- Geckos have no eyelids. To keep their eyeballs wet, they lick them with their tongues.

- A giraffe's tongue is almost 2 feet long. A giraffe uses its tongue to clean its own ears!
- Why do dogs have wet noses? A dog's nose gets wet because of mucus and other fluids draining out of it. Dogs often wet their noses with their tongues, too. Slimy noses may seem disgusting, but they actually mean the dog is healthy. It's only when a dog is feverish or dehydrated that its nose won't produce as much mucus and becomes dry and hot.
- Some breeds of dog drool when they get excited. An excited mastiff or boxer might have ropes of slimy drool hanging out of its mouth!
- Camels and llamas spit when they get angry. Camel spit is actually a slimy wad of mucus. A camel spitball can weigh almost half a pound. That's a lot of slime!
- The poison-arrow frog's body is covered with a slimy poison that paralyzes anything that touches it. One of these little creatures has enough poison on its body to kill 2,000 people. That makes it one of the most poisonous creatures on Earth. South America's native tribes used to put the poison on their arrows to make their weapons even more deadly.
- A lizard called the horned toad scares away enemies by squirting blood out of its eyes.
- The spitting cobra spits venom into its enemies' eyes.
- Not many things smell worse than skunk spray, right? Then why is a liquid called musk, which is found in

skunk spray, the main ingredient in many perfumes and aftershaves?

 Fish scales are used to make lipstick.

- Komodo dragons have one of the nastiest mouths in the animal world. This lizard's saliva is so full of bacteria and germs, it can actually kill another animal. That's because a bite from a Komodo dragon often becomes infected. After the bitten animal dies, the Komodo dragon finds the body and eats it. Death by slime!

- Bird droppings are actually urine and excrement mixed together. The bird's body removes almost all of the liquid from its waste, leaving a white material called uric acid.

- The excrement of some seabirds and bats is called guano. Some people collect guano, because it makes a terrific fertilizer.

Your Slimy Stomach

Uh-oh. You don't feel well. Your stomach is churning. Quick, run to the bathroom! You're going to throw up!

People (and animals) vomit when something irritates their stomachs. Sometimes that something is a virus or a nasty bacteria that makes us sick. Other times, it's something bad in our food or a food that our body just doesn't like. Whatever the reason, vomiting is an awfully slimy way to get rid of what's bothering our stomachs!

What is vomit, anyway? Most of it is food that our stomachs haven't digested yet. But there's lots of other icky stuff in it, too.

Vomit is slimy because it's full of mucus from your stomach. Your stomach contains lots of important digestive juices that help break down your food. There's also plenty of mucus down there to coat your stomach walls and protect them from the strong acids that help you digest. Your stomach produces more than a quart of digestive juices every day.

When you throw up, you also regurgitate a greenish liquid called bile. Bile is made by your liver and found in your small intestine. It helps digest fats and other parts of your food.

Vomiting is an involuntary reaction. Once your body decides it needs to vomit, nothing can stop it. It may be difficult to appreciate, but it's just your body's way of returning to better health.

Take a Peek Inside

Here's an incredible, but true, stomach story. In the early 1800s, a young Canadian named Alexis St. Martin accidentally shot himself in the side. The injury left a big hole in his stomach. Fortunately Alexis survived, but the hole in his stomach never healed. Alexis covered the hole with a bandage and somehow managed to live a pretty normal life.

A doctor named William Beaumont treated Alexis. This "window" inside the human body fascinated Dr. Beaumont, and he asked Alexis if he could conduct a few experiments. Alexis said yes, and Dr. Beaumont started doing some weird scientific things. In one experiment, he tied a string around a piece of raw meat and put it into Alexis's stomach. Later, he pulled the meat out and saw that it was partly digested.

Dr. Beaumont also tested the fluids in Alexis's stomach. He discovered that digestive juices contain lots of hydrochloric acid, which helps to break down food (and pretty much anything else it touches—hydrochloric acid is strong stuff). Dr. Beaumont even drank some of Alexis's stomach slime to see what it tasted like. Yuck! That was one experiment the doctor tried only once.

Dr. Beaumont studied Alexis's stomach for eleven years. Then, in 1833, he published his results. Dr.

Beaumont became famous from his work. Back then, people didn't know much about how the digestive system worked. Dr. Beaumont's experiments on Alexis's see-through stomach added much important information to the medical world.

Spit Out Some Slime

If you think your stomach is a slimy place, check out your mouth. Every day, your mouth produces more than a quart of saliva, or spit. That works out to about 6,000 gallons in a lifetime—enough to fill hundreds of bathtubs.

Saliva is almost all water. But there's other stuff floating around in there, too, including chemicals that help you break down food.

Tiny glands inside your cheeks and under your tongue create saliva. These glands spend all their time producing

spit and pouring it into your mouth. You use that spit to make your food easier to swallow.

Did you know there are lots of tiny creatures swimming around in your saliva? These creatures are called microorganisms. Their job is to kill nasty bacteria that might make you sick or rot your teeth. There are about 300 different kinds of microorganisms in your mouth—up to 150 million little creatures at a time!

Do You Have a Slimy Nose?

Is your nose running? When you sneeze, does slime fly out of your nose? That drippy slime is actually mucus. And even though it sometimes seems disgusting, mucus has an important job.

Your nose produces more than a quart of mucus every day. Usually, this mucus is clear and kind of sticky. Its job is to capture dust and dirt from the air you breathe and prevent it from going into your lungs. After a while, the mucus flows to the back of your nose and then down your throat into your stomach. So nose slime is actually part of your diet!

If you've ever had a bad cold, you've probably noticed that your nose mucus is sometimes yellow or green instead of clear. These colors come from bacteria in your nose. During a cold, the mucus in your nose also becomes thicker. You have to keep blowing your nose and sneezing to get that goopy slime out of your head.

Speaking of sneezing, did you know?

- Sneezes fly out of your nose and mouth faster than 100 miles per hour.
- It's impossible to keep your eyes open when you sneeze.

Slimy Bumps

You went on a ten-mile hike, and now there's a small lump on your foot where it rubbed against your sneaker. Or you touched something really hot and a squishy bump popped up on your burned finger. If you poke these bumps with something sharp, they'll pop and a clear liquid will flow out. These tender bumps are called blisters.

Blisters form when something—such as a rubbing sneaker or a hot pot—damages your skin. When your

skin is rubbed raw or burned, the injury can cause a tiny tear under the surface. Fluids leak from the damaged tissues but have nowhere to escape. So they form a bubble under the surface of your skin. The skin puffs up and there it is—a blister. Sometimes an injury will cause a blister to fill with blood, forming a blood blister. You can see the red blood through the skin. Blisters also form when you get sick with the chicken pox and some other illnesses.

Blisters usually go away by themselves in a few days as the skin heals and the liquids drain back into the body. Sometimes, if blisters are large and painful, people pop them with a sterilized needle. However, popping a blister can lead to infection. And then you'll have another kind of slime to deal with. This nasty slime is called pus.

Pus Power

Pus is mostly made of water and body fluids. However, there are icky things in pus, too, such as dead bacteria and dead white blood cells that sacrificed themselves to fight the infection. The dead bacteria and blood cells smell bad and make the pus look yellow or green.

Pus is a sign of infection. If you have pus coming out of a cut, blister, insect bite, or other injury, it's time to see a doctor.

Pus is also the goopy stuff inside pimples.

Another place you find pus is inside boils. Boils are really big pimples deep under your skin. They form when glands in your skin get blocked and infected. Boils can be painful. Sometimes a doctor lances, or cuts open, a boil with a sharp knife. That allows all the slimy pus to gush out and helps clear up the infection.

Slimy Eyes

Do your eyes ever feel gooey or crusty when you wake up in the morning? Do you look in the mirror and see a bit of glop around your eyes? Don't worry. Everyone wakes up looking like this.

Why are your eyes slimy in the morning? During the day, tiny ducts in your eyes produce tears to keep your eyes moist and clean. Tears are made of water, mucus, chemicals, and a little bit of oil. You hardly notice these tears, because they drain out of your eyes through small tubes into your nose. Then the tears go down your throat when you swallow. But at night, it's a different story.

When your eyes are closed, the little drainage holes are closed, too. That means your tears can't get into your nose. Instead, they gather at the corners of your eyes. Most of the liquid dries up during the night. You're left with crusty gunk to greet you in the morning. Fortunately, it's perfectly normal.

Eyes are pretty slimy places. A slippery jelly surrounds your eyeball to keep it clean and protect it from dirt. Add that to all the tears floating around, and your eyes are a wet and hard-working place!

Sweaty Slime

Did you know that your body is covered in slime? Almost every square inch of your skin is full of sweat glands. The palm of your hand alone has more than two thousand of these slime-producing glands. You lose about a quart of liquid through your sweat glands every day. This liquid is a combination of water, salt, and a waste material called urea.

Sweat can be pretty stinky. Fortunately, only certain parts of the body produce smelly sweat. The worst offenders are the armpits and the feet. Bacteria love to live in these dark, moist places. The bacteria mix with the sweat and make it smell unpleasant.

Why do people sweat? Sweating may make you feel gross, but it's an important way to control your body temperature. You've probably noticed that you sweat on a hot day, or if you're exercising or wearing too many warm clothes. The hotter you get, the more you sweat. Sweat lies on your skin and cools the surface of your body. That allows your body heat to escape into the air. You could say sweat is a kind of slimy air conditioning!

Make Your Own Slime

Here are two cool slimes you can make at home.

Slime-Making Tips

Wear old clothing when handling slime, and don't use slime near upholstered furniture. It may stain fabrics. Don't put slime in your mouth, and wash your hands after you finish. Store your slime in a resealable plastic bag to prevent it from drying out.

Basic Slime

Ingredients:
- 1¼ cups water
- 1 tablespoon borax (available in the laundry section of your grocery store)
- ¼ cup white craft glue
- resealable plastic bag
- food coloring

Directions:
1. Mix 1 cup of water with the borax. Stir until the borax is completely dissolved.
2. Mix the remaining ¼ cup of water with the craft glue.
3. Combine the borax solution and glue solution in the resealable plastic bag. Add a few drops of food coloring.
4. Seal the bag and knead the mixture until you have a thick gel. You can store the slime in its bag in the refrigerator when you are done playing with it.

NOTE: THIS SLIME IS NOT EDIBLE. DO NOT TASTE IT OR FEED IT TO YOUR LITTLE BROTHER, THE DOG, OR ANYONE ELSE!

Goopy Slime

NOTE: THIS RECIPE REQUIRES USING A STOVE. ASK AN ADULT TO HELP OR SUPERVISE.

Ingredients:

- 2 cups water
- ½ cup cornstarch
- food coloring

Directions:

1. Place the water in a saucepan over medium heat. Bring to a boil. (Ask an adult to help or supervise.) Stir in the cornstarch and mix well.
2. Add a few drops of food coloring and mix well.
3. Remove from the heat and let your slime cool before playing with it. You can store the slime in a resealable plastic bag.

NOTE: THIS SLIME IS NOT EDIBLE. DO NOT TASTE IT OR FEED IT TO YOUR LITTLE SISTER, THE CAT, OR ANYONE ELSE!

Slime on the Web

There are lots of slimy sites on the Internet. Here are just a few where you can get slimed.

Grossology, the Science of Really Gross Things
www.grossology.org
You won't believe all the slimy facts and fun you'll find at this site!

Mad Sci Network
www.madsci.org
Includes a slime recipe, as well as lots of other wacky science experiments and fun projects.

"Nature's Slimy Friends"/American Museum of Natural History
www.amnh.org/nationalcenter/youngnaturalistawards/1998/slimy.html
This lively article about slugs is full of fascinating information.

Slimy Science Experiments
www.yahooligans.com/science_and_nature/Experiments_and_Activities/
Check out this search engine for lots of slimy science fun.

You Can't Do That on Television
www.ycdtotv.com/swp/recipes.html
A huge variety of slime recipes.